CORNERSTONES of FREEDOM™

WORLD WAR I

BY JOSH GREGORY

CHILDREN'S PRESS®

An Imprint of Scholastic Inc.

New York   Toronto   London   Auckland   Sydney

Mexico City   New Delhi   Hong Kong

Danbury, Connecticut

BRINGING HISTORY to LIFE

Content Consultant
James Marten, PhD
Professor and Chair, History Department
Marquette University
Milwaukee, Wisconsin

Library of Congress Cataloging-in-Publication Data
Gregory, Josh.
   World War I/by Josh Gregory.
      p. cm.—(Cornerstones of freedom)
   Includes bibliographical references and index.
   ISBN-13: 978-0-531-23068-8 (lib. bdg.)   ISBN-10: 0-531-23068-6 (lib. bdg.)
   ISBN-13: 978-0-531-28168-0 (pbk.)   ISBN-10: 0-531-28168-X (pbk.)
   1. World War, 1914–1918—Juvenile literature. I. Title. II. Title:
World War One. III. Series.
   D522.7.G74 2012
   940.3—dc23   2011031128

1 2 3 4 5 6 7 8 9 10 R 21 20 19 18 17 16 15 14 13 12

Photographs © 2012: age fotostock: cover (The Board of Trustees), 22
(Universal History Arc); AP Images: 49 (Donald Stampfli), back cover, 11;
Getty Images: 5 top, 16 (Alinari Archives, Florence), 32 (Central Press),
47 (FPG/Hulton Archive), 46 (Henry Guttmann), 39 (Hulton Archive), 55
(Keystone), 54 (Mansell/Time & Life Pictures), 13 (Paul Thompson/FPG);
Granger Collection: 6 (Rue des Archives), 5 bottom, 19, 26, 28, 58 (ullstein
bild), 23, 30, 31, 57 top; Library of Congress: 4 top, 7 (Detroit Photographic
Company), 50 (Edward Jackson/Bain News Service), 45, 57 bottom
(Soyuzfoto), 42, 59 (Vladimir Aleksandrovich Serov); Courtesy of Naval
History and Heritage Command: 10; North Wind Picture Archives: 12;
Superstock, Inc.: 2, 3, 14, 18 (De Agostini), 17, 40 (Everett Collection), 41
(Universal Images Group); The Image Works: 8 (Alexander Richardson/
Science Museum/SSPL), 24 (Jacques Boyer/Roger-Viollet), 4 bottom, 15
(Mary Evans Picture Library), 20, 36, 48 (Mary Evans/Robert Hunt Collection),
25 (Mary Evans/Robert Hunt Collection/Imperial War Museum), 44 (Roger-
Viollet), 34 (SZ Photo/Scherl); Woodrow Wilson Presidential Library: 38, 56.

Maps by XNR Productions, Inc.

Did you know that studying history can be fun?

BRING HISTORY TO LIFE by becoming a history investigator. Examine the evidence (primary and secondary source materials); cross-examine the people and witnesses. Take a look at what was happening at the time—but be careful! What happened years ago might suddenly become incredibly interesting and change the way you think!

Contents

SETTING THE SCENE
Rising Tension............6

CHAPTER 1
Worldwide Conflict.......8

CHAPTER 2
Off to War.................20

CHAPTER 3
The Fight Continues.................32

CHAPTER 4
Working Toward Peace......................42

4

MAP OF THE EVENTS
What Happened Where?..................... 52

THE STORY CONTINUES
A Changed World........ 54

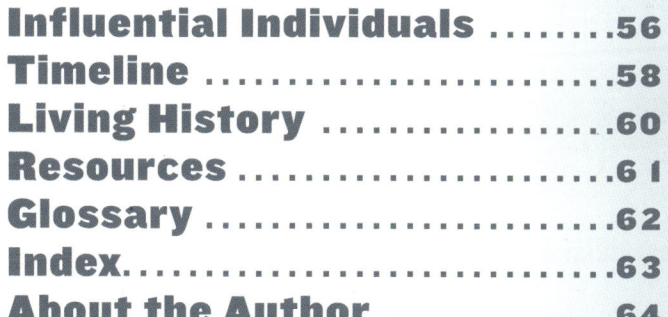

Influential Individuals 56

Timeline 58

Living History 60

Resources 61

Glossary 62

Index..............................63

About the Author..............64

Rising Tension

Great Britain established colonies in India in the 1600s.

By the late 1800s, several of Europe's most powerful nations had expanded into empires with colonies around the world. Countries such as Great Britain, Germany, France, and Russia controlled large portions of land in Africa, Asia, and elsewhere. They used these colonies to increase their economic power. Many colonies produced

MODERN NATIONS SUCH AS POLAND WERE PART

important raw materials such as food, cotton, and oil. Some European leaders believed that such colonies would provide a secure future for their nations. As European empires grew larger and more powerful, they began to compete for territory. Each nation wanted to become the greatest power in the world.

The competing nations soon began to form rivalries and **alliances**. By the early 1900s, Germany had formed a close alliance with its southern neighbor, Austria-Hungary. Its eastern neighbor, Russia, had claimed much of eastern Europe for itself. The western nations of Great Britain, France, and Italy each maintained large empires. All of these countries would soon become caught up in a worldwide struggle for control of Europe. This struggle would result in the bloodiest war the world had ever seen.

The Algerian capital city of Algiers was the center of France's colonial empire in Africa.

CHAPTER I

WORLDWIDE CONFLICT

Large warships were constructed in British factories in the early 1900s.

SIGNS OF THE COMING WAR

began to appear in the early 1900s. The rivalry between the empires helped start a major arms race among them. New technology allowed countries to construct weapons unlike any that had been used before. Each country continually worked to beat the others in a competition to create more powerful weapons. Though none of the countries was at war, they began to stockpile, or gather, large amounts of weapons and war vehicles.

The HMS *Dreadnought* was more powerful than any warship built before it.

The Naval Arms Race

In 1906, Great Britain had the largest navy in the world. That year, the British launched a massive new battleship called the HMS *Dreadnought*. The ship was both very large and very fast. It was equipped with dozens of large guns and several torpedo tubes for launching underwater missiles. At the time, it was the most powerful battleship in the world.

Germany did not have a strong navy in 1906. But the Germans did not want to be outdone by the British. They soon began constructing their own ships like the *Dreadnought*. These new ships were more heavily armed than the British ships and were clearly designed to travel the distance to Great Britain, but no farther. The British responded by increasing their own ship production. They had the resources to create ships faster than Germany could. The British began building at a rate of about two ships for every one built by Germany.

German admiral Alfred von Tirpitz was one of the biggest supporters of Germany's naval buildup in the years leading to World War I.

Germany's desire to build up a large navy came at the expense of its land army. In the years leading up to World War I, the country spent a full one-third of its military budget on its navy. These heavy costs were taken directly out of the army budget. As a result, Germany's army was small for a nation with its population. Germany's population was about 65 million at the time. France's was just 40 million. Yet the two countries' armies were about the same size.

Kaiser Wilhelm II was the emperor of Germany during World War I.

Alliances

Around this time, major European powers began to form the alliances that would dictate the course of the war. Russia, Great Britain, and France promised one another to intervene if Germany attacked any of them. They hoped that this would prevent Germany from trying to expand into their territory. In 1912, Germany, Austria-Hungary, and Italy agreed to renew a Triple Alliance that had originally been formed in 1882.

Russia controlled much of eastern Europe, including the territory along Germany's eastern border. As Germany became more powerful, its leaders began hoping to conquer some of this Russian territory for their own empire. But the German leaders knew that attacking without an excuse would result in Russia's allies joining the fight. They decided to wait for a better opportunity to attack.

A Reason for War

Turkish rulers controlled an empire in southeast Europe and the Middle East. This was known as the Ottoman Empire. During the Balkan Wars of 1912 and 1913, the Balkan nations of Serbia, Bulgaria, Greece, and Montenegro fought to take over the European portion of the Ottoman Empire. They won the territory, but Serbia and Montenegro were forced by neighboring Austria-Hungary and Italy to give up parts of their newly won land. That territory would then form the independent nation of Albania. The Serbians were upset by this action. Many of them saw Austria-Hungary as an enemy. Some even began plotting to strike their northern neighbor.

Bulgaria was one of several countries that fought against Turkey during the Balkan Wars.

Archduke Ferdinand and his wife were shot while riding in a car.

One Serbian group decided to **assassinate** Archduke Franz Ferdinand. Ferdinand was next in line for the Austrian throne. The Serbian group learned that Ferdinand was scheduled to visit Sarajevo, Bosnia, in June 1914. Bosnia was a part of the Austro-Hungarian Empire, but it was home to many Serbs. Ferdinand would be visiting to inspect military facilities.

On June 28, Ferdinand and his wife were shot and killed by a young Bosnian Serb named Gavrilo Princip. Little did Princip know that his actions would mark the beginning of a massive world war.

Austria-Hungary did not want to let this crime go unpunished. They began making plans for an attack on Serbia. Germany saw this as a perfect opportunity to attack Russia, which was sure to enter the battle in support of Serbia. Russia had supported Serbia and its neighbors in several conflicts against Turkey and Austria. Russian leaders knew that they would not be taken seriously in further engagements in the region if they did not continue to support Serbia. Kaiser Wilhelm II of Germany promised Austria-Hungary that Germany would support it if it began a war against Serbia.

SPOTLIGHT ON

Franz Ferdinand

Franz Ferdinand was born on December 18, 1863, in Graz, Austria. He was the nephew of Austrian emperor Franz Josef. The emperor's only son, Rudolf, killed himself in 1889. This made Ferdinand's father the heir to the throne. Ferdinand became heir when his father died in 1896.

Ferdinand began to play an important role in the Austrian military during the early 1900s. He was made inspector general of the Austrian army in 1913. He was assassinated the following year.

Austria-Hungary created an excuse for war by issuing Serbia an **ultimatum** that Serbia was sure to refuse. The ultimatum was issued on July 23. It demanded that Serbia publicly apologize to Austria-Hungary for the assassination

Austria-Hungary's ultimatum to Serbia caught worldwide attention. It made the front page of the *New York Times* on July 23, 1914. Most readers probably had no idea that the event would eventually lead to such a massive conflict. See page 60 for a link to view the original article online.

and promise to punish and suppress any future acts against Austria-Hungary, among other conditions. Two days later, Serbia accepted all but two of the conditions and offered to negotiate. Austria-Hungary responded by closing off diplomacy and declaring war on July 28. The declaration set off a chain of events that would soon draw countries around the world into conflict.

The Austrian newspaper *Wiener Zeitung* printed a special edition on July 28, 1914, announcing the declaration of war against Serbia.

The Serbian military marched toward Serbia's border with Austria, but did not have the means to defend itself on its own.

The War Begins

Austrian forces attacked the Serbian capital city of Belgrade the day after declaring war. Just as the Germans had predicted, Russia began mobilizing troops to support Serbia almost immediately. Germany sent an ultimatum to Russia demanding that it call off the attack. It also sent one to France demanding that it remain neutral during the conflict. Germany did not receive an answer from either country.

German forces entered Belgium soon after the outbreak of war.

On August 1, Germany declared war on Russia. France responded by mobilizing troops against Germany. To stage a proper attack on France, Germany knew it would need to cross through Belgium. The French-German border was too well defended to attack directly. Germany demanded on August 2 that Belgium allow German troops to pass through freely on their way to France.

Belgium was an ally of Great Britain. The Germans knew that an attack on Belgium was likely to draw Britain into the war. Yet they still chose to invade Belgium on August 3 after being denied free passage through the country. Germany also declared war on France that same day. Great Britain had no choice but to declare war against Germany the following day. Serbia, Montenegro, and Japan also joined the fight against Germany and Austria-Hungary by the end of August. Despite its Triple Alliance with Germany and Austria-Hungary, Italy chose to remain neutral.

On September 5, 1914, the three major Allied powers made their alliance official. Russia, Great Britain, and France all agreed that none of them would make a separate peace agreement with Germany and Austria-Hungary's Central powers. They would fight together until the war's end.

YESTERDAY'S HEADLINES

When the war first began, most people believed that it would be over quickly. Many people predicted that the troops would be "home for Christmas." They did not expect the long, bloody conflict that was to come. As a result, there was widespread support for the war in all of the countries involved. Each nation believed that it would be victorious. Great waves of patriotism swept across Europe.

Another result of these expectations was that military leaders threw all of their resources into the war right as it began. They had no idea that they would still be fighting more than four years later.

CHAPTER 2

OFF TO WAR

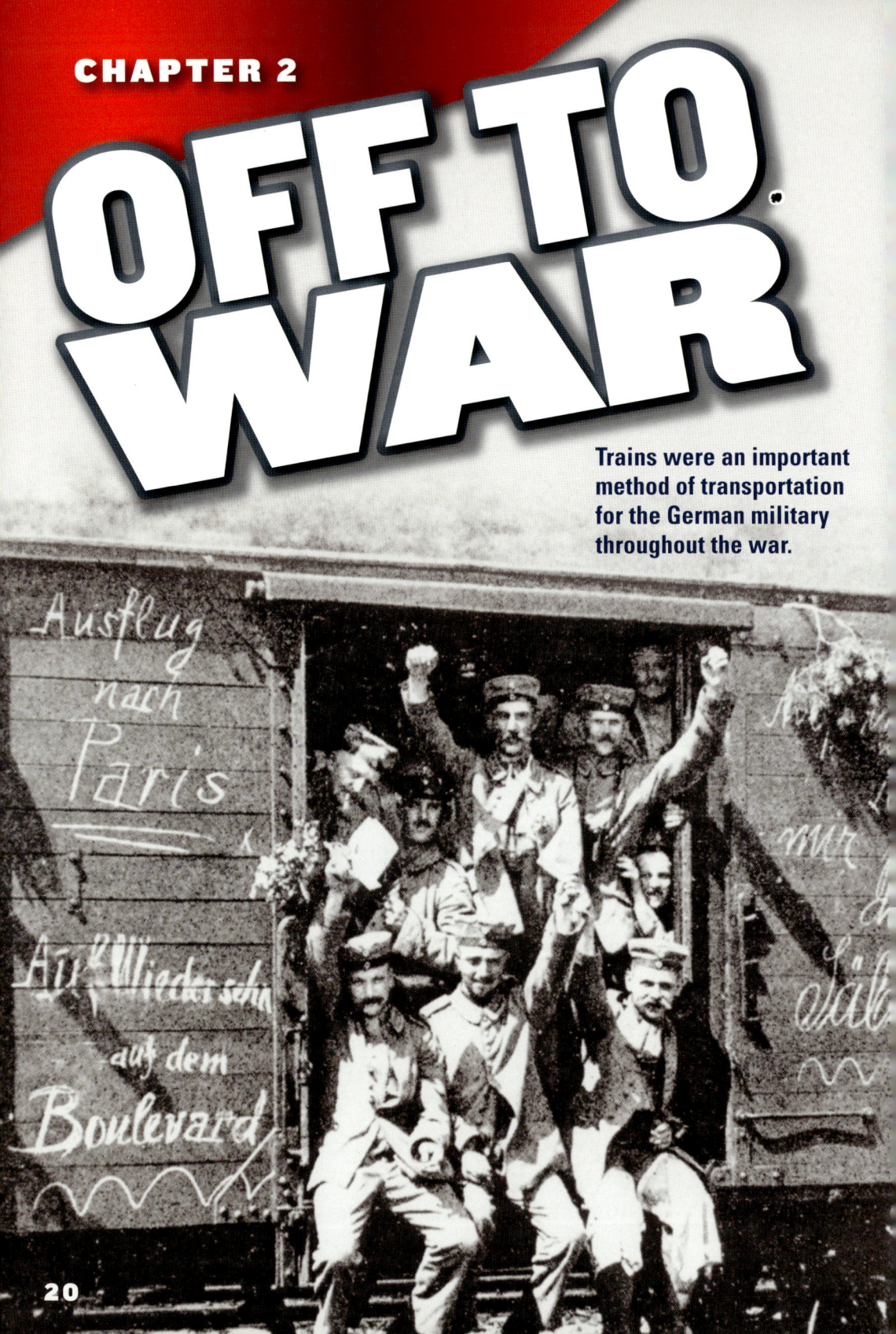

Trains were an important method of transportation for the German military throughout the war.

The Allies had several

advantages over their enemies as the war began. Between them, they had many more soldiers than the Central powers. Germany and Austria-Hungary had a combined total of about 2.5 million soldiers. The Allies had well over 3 million. They also had the advantage of location. The Central powers truly were central. They were caught in between France and Great Britain to the west and Russia to the east. But the Central powers had their own advantages as well. Their railroads made it easy for them to move troops quickly. Russia especially would have trouble keeping up with this rapid transportation throughout the war.

Alfred von Schlieffen's plan called for a relentless opening assault.

The Schlieffen Plan

Germany knew that it would be difficult to fight a war on two **fronts**. But the long buildup of tension in Europe had encouraged the German military to start planning for such an event years before the war began. German officer Alfred von Schlieffen began preparing a strategy for a two-front war in the 1890s. He continued working on it up until his retirement in 1905. Schlieffen was replaced by Helmuth von Moltke, who saw the value of the Schlieffen Plan.

As the war began, Moltke began working to update the plan. The basic idea of the plan was to quickly defeat France while staying defensive on the eastern front. To do this, the plan called for two armies to attack on the western front. One would launch a heavy attack on

France from the north, through Belgium. The other would then move into France from the south while the French forces were busy with the northern attack.

Moltke made several changes to the plan that caused it to become less effective. The southern army was supposed to stay where it was until the northern forces had moved into France. But Moltke allowed parts of the southern army to begin early offensive strikes. He moved troops from the northern army to reinforce the southern army. He also sent troops from the western front across the country to the eastern front. This greatly weakened the armies attacking France. The Schlieffen Plan had been based on a strong opening attack. Moltke's changes caused it to fall apart.

SPOTLIGHT ON

Helmuth von Moltke

Helmuth von Moltke was born in Germany on May 25, 1848. His uncle was a high-ranking officer in the German military. Moltke joined the army at a young age and began working directly under his uncle in 1882. He rose through the ranks quickly and replaced Alfred von Schlieffen as chief of the German General Staff in 1906. He was removed from this position almost immediately after the German loss at the Marne. His changes to the Schlieffen Plan were seen as the major cause of Germany's failures in the beginning of the war.

The First Battle of the Marne

The Germans were able to make their way through Belgium and into France by early September 1914, even though their army had weakened. They had the French troops on the retreat and were nearing Paris. French general Joseph Joffre saw an opportunity to turn the tide. He ordered one army to launch a counterattack against the Germans near the banks of the Marne River on September 6. It was an immediate success. The German troops were quickly split into two separate groups. This would likely not have happened if Moltke had not moved troops away from the northern army. A combined force of British and French troops was able to move in between the two German groups. The Germans began a retreat into Belgium after four days of combat.

Powerful artillery shells helped the French and British forces win the Battle of the Marne.

Much of the war was fought from trenches.

In September, both the Allies and the Germans began to dig the war's first **trenches** along the western front. These front lines would move little throughout the war. Instead of quickly defeating France, Germany had caused a **stalemate** to the west. It would be forced to fight on two fronts for the rest of the war.

The Eastern Front

Russia began combat on the eastern front with an early push into northeastern Germany. Two armies invaded Germany in late August. They were led by Russian generals Paul von Rennenkampf and Alexander

Russia suffered heavy losses at the Battle of Tannenberg.

Samsonov. They separated and lost contact with one another as they progressed into foreign territory. Rennenkampf was able to win a small battle. Samsonov was not so lucky. Germany launched a massive attack against his army on August 26 near the town of Tannenberg. Samsonov lost more than half of his men. German forces captured 92,000 Russians and killed or wounded 30,000 others. The Germans lost only 13,000 of their own men. The terrible loss led Samsonov to shoot and kill himself on August 29. It was a major victory for Germany. German forces did not move any farther east, but they caused serious damage to the Russian military.

The Dardanelles Campaign

Late October saw the entrance of yet another country into the war. Turkish ships joined German forces in a series of attacks on Russian ports on October 29 and 30. By November 5, each of the Allied forces had declared war on Turkey.

Turkey lay across the Black Sea to the south of Russia. Russia was soon forced to deal with both Turkish attacks from the south and German attacks along the eastern front. In January 1915, Russia requested that its allies begin an attack on Turkey. French and British naval fleets began the attack on February 19, focusing on the Dardanelles channel to the northwest of Turkey. Land combat began on April 25. The campaign continued throughout the year. By the end of 1915, Allied leaders realized that there was no way to win without bringing in massive reinforcements. They could not afford to focus so many troops on the campaign. They withdrew in early 1916. There were more than 200,000 Allied **casualties** during the campaign, but no real gain was made.

A FIRSTHAND LOOK AT
WORLD WAR I PHOTOS

Many photographs were taken during the war. They offer a close look at what life was like for soldiers fighting in the trenches. They also show just how much damage the war caused to many European towns. See page 60 for a link to view some of these photographs online.

The sinking of the RMS *Lusitania* showed that Germany was willing to attack even civilian ships in the effort to enforce its blockade on Great Britain.

The War Grows Larger

The Allies began working in early 1915 to gain Italy's support in the war. Italy had previously agreed to be part of the Triple Alliance with Germany and Austria-Hungary. But its leaders also wanted to take control of certain parts of Austrian territory. The Allies agreed to let Italy take over part of Austria-Hungary in exchange for its support in the war. The Treaty of London was signed on April 26, 1915. It added Italy to the growing number of Allied nations. Italy officially declared war on Austria-Hungary on May 23.

The Sinking of the *Lusitania*

In February, Germany had declared a **blockade** on Great Britain. Germany promised that its submarines, called U-boats, would attack any ship traveling into Great Britain. The Germans were true to their word. On May 7, U-boats attacked the ocean liner *Lusitania* as it attempted to return to Liverpool from New York City. Almost 2,000 civilians were on the ship. One hundred and twenty-eight of them were U.S. citizens. German torpedoes sunk the ship in an attack that lasted less than 20 minutes. Almost 1,200 people were killed. The Germans claimed that the attack was justified because the *Lusitania* had been carrying ammunition into Great Britain.

A VIEW FROM ABROAD

The sinking of the *Lusitania* outraged many people in the United States. It was widely assumed that the United States would declare war on Germany in response. But the country remained neutral even after Germany sunk two more ships carrying U.S. passengers. President Woodrow Wilson made it clear that he was committed to avoiding U.S. involvement in the war. He responded to the submarine attacks with diplomacy rather than combat. On May 13, President Wilson sent a letter to the German government to protest the *Lusitania* attack and demand that Germany be more careful in the future. He issued a similar protest after the sinking of the *Arabic* in August.

Czar Nicholas II's (second from right) decision to take direct control of Russia's military would eventually prove disastrous.

U-boats attacked another ship, the *Arabic*, on August 17. Like the *Lusitania*, the *Arabic* carried many U.S. civilians. The U.S. government issued a protest against Germany. German officials promised to be more careful in selecting targets. But on September 18, their submarines sank yet another ocean liner. Germany decided soon after to call off the submarine blockade to avoid drawing the United States into the war.

The Czar

On September 5, Czar Nicholas II, the emperor of Russia, took control of his country's military. Many Russians greeted this news with displeasure. Nicholas did not have any military experience. Government officials advised against his decision. The czar responded by dismissing them from their positions. He left the capital and went to the front, where he could keep a close eye on the war's progress. Political decisions back home were left in the hands of Nicholas's wife, Alexandra. Alexandra was heavily influenced by a man named Grigory Yefimovich Rasputin. Rasputin was able to ease the pain of the czar's sickly son. Alexandra believed Rasputin to be a holy man because of this. She kept him close and trusted his advice. While Nicholas was focused on the war, Alexandra replaced many government officials with less capable ones chosen by Rasputin. The acts inspired negative views of Nicholas throughout the country. Russia's government would not remain stable for much longer.

Rasputin (seated) had a major influence on Russia's government.

CHAPTER 3

THE FIGHT CONTINUES

The British military required a constant stream of new recruits throughout the war.

THE WAR REMAINED AT A standstill at the beginning of 1916. Hundreds of thousands of men had died on both sides of the conflict. But neither side had much to show for the loss. The front lines had moved little. World leaders realized that the war would not be over as quickly as they had originally predicted. In January 1916, Great Britain began a **conscription** program for its military. It had previously been the only country fighting the war with a volunteer army. Many British men had signed up to join the military. But it was not enough. Great Britain would need many more soldiers if it wanted to help the Allies achieve victory.

German forces pressed forward at Verdun, France, despite defensive attacks from French artillery.

The Battle of Verdun

The war's single longest battle began in February. German forces led by General Erich von Falkenhayn began gathering **artillery** in huge numbers near France's Verdun fortress. French leaders noticed the buildup of German forces near the fort. But they did not believe that the Germans would attack the fortress itself. They instead began preparing to defend other locations nearby. The French soldiers were caught off guard when Germany attacked the fortress on February 21.

Reinforcements led by French general Henri Philippe Pétain hurried to help defend Verdun.

The German forces continued pushing forward for several months. They made great progress and captured smaller forts as they went. But they were unable to capture Verdun itself. The German advance came to an end in July, when French forces were finally able to begin pushing the Germans back. France continued to attack for the rest of the year. This offensive campaign resulted in France regaining all of its territory by December. Over a million men were killed or wounded during the long battle.

The Battle of Jutland

There was only one major sea battle throughout the course of the war. The British and German navies had threatened one another for several years. They finally clashed in the North Sea not far from Jutland, Denmark, on May 31. British leaders received word that the German High Seas Fleet was leaving port across the sea from Great Britain. They began preparing for an attack. Soon, the British came into contact with a small German scouting fleet. The British fleet chased the scouting ships as they fled back to the main German fleet. A massive naval battle took place. Both sides suffered enormous damage, but the Germans harmed the British fleet more than they were harmed themselves. Still, the British naval forces were able to force the Germans back and hold on to control of the North Sea. Both sides saw the battle as a victory.

The Somme Campaign

On June 24, British soldiers began launching artillery shells into German trenches along the Somme River in France. They launched almost two million shells over the course of one week. On July 1, they began moving **infantry** forward toward the German lines. The German trenches were protected well. Walls of barbed wire blocked the British soldiers' path as German machine guns mowed them down. More than 19,000 British troops died in a single day. Almost 40,000 more were injured. Yet the British continued their push forward.

Allied troops used trenches to advance toward the German lines.

They suffered about 158,000 casualties in the first month of the campaign.

On September 15, the British brought tanks into the war for the first time. The tanks helped the British move forward and recapture two villages. But they were unsuccessful overall. Muddy, uneven ground made it difficult to travel. Many tanks and soldiers became stuck and were unable to continue moving forward. The Somme campaign finally ended on November 13. Great Britain had managed to push the lines forward only about 5 miles (8 kilometers). This small gain cost hundreds of thousands of casualties on both sides. Great Britain lost about 420,000 men. France lost around 200,000. Germany lost between 500,000 and 650,000.

New Leaders and Major Developments

Across the ocean, Woodrow Wilson had been reelected president on November 7. His campaign slogan had been "He kept us out of the war." Great Britain received a new leader exactly one month later, when David Lloyd George was elected prime minister. In Russia, things continued to go poorly for Czar Nicholas and his family. Relatives of the czar had grown tired of Rasputin and his influence over Alexandra. They murdered Rasputin on December 30. Despite this, people were still unhappy with Nicholas.

In January 1917, Germany began an attempt to persuade Mexico to attack the United States. Mexico and the United States had a tense relationship at the

Woodrow Wilson

Woodrow Wilson was the 28th president of the United States. He was born in 1856 in Staunton, Virginia. Wilson suffered from a learning disability and did not learn to read until he was 10 years old. He did not let this stop his education. He eventually earned a doctorate in government and history, and wrote several books about U.S. politics. He was named the president of Princeton University in 1902 and became the governor of New Jersey eight years later. His leadership made him an excellent candidate for U.S. president in 1912. As president, Wilson led the country through the war and helped to pass the 19th Amendment, which allowed women to vote.

time. The current Mexican government had recently come to power because of a revolution. But President Wilson had refused to recognize the new government. Later in January, British intelligence discovered a letter from the German foreign secretary that detailed Germany's proposal.

Unaware of this, President Wilson called for a "peace without victory" on January 22. He hoped to convince the warring nations to abandon the fight. But Germany returned to its policy of unrestricted submarine attacks on British waters on February 1. Wilson ended U.S. diplomatic relations with Germany two days later. Soon after, the British revealed the secret deal Germany was trying to make with Mexico. The information was released to the

Violence broke out in the streets of Petrograd, Russia, in March 1917.

public on March 1. A demand for war began to spread throughout the United States in response.

In Russia, Czar Nicholas lost power completely in March 1917. People throughout the country were unhappy with his leadership and Russia's lack of progress in the war. There had been major losses of troops with no real gain. The Russian economy had suffered greatly as well. On March 8, riots over food shortages broke out in the capital city of Petrograd. Soon, even the Russian soldiers stationed in the city began to join in. On March 15, Nicholas was forced to give up the throne. A temporary government was set up to rule the country until a more permanent choice could be made. Nicholas and his family were imprisoned. Their

A FIRSTHAND LOOK AT
TRUMAN'S WORLD WAR I LETTERS

Future U.S. president Harry S. Truman was one of many American soldiers who fought in Europe during World War I. He wrote many letters home to his future wife, Bess. They offer a firsthand account of life in the trenches. See page 60 for a link to read the letters online.

captors murdered them in July 1918 when supporters of the czar attempted to rescue the family.

Soon after the 1917 revolution in Russia, the United States finally ran out of patience for Germany's actions. On April 6, the United States declared war on Germany. The decision to support the Allied forces would mark a major

On April 2, 1917, President Wilson asked Congress to declare war, and they did so four days later.

turning point in the war. The United States was able to provide its allies with much-needed money and supplies. It would eventually loan more than $7 billion to the various Allied nations through the course of the war. It was also able to provide food shipments to Allied troops.

U.S. entry into the war inspired many other countries to join against the Central powers. Several Central and South American nations followed the United States' lead by 1918. On May 18, the U.S. government passed the Selective Service Act. This act began conscription in the United States. The first U.S. forces arrived in France on June 26.

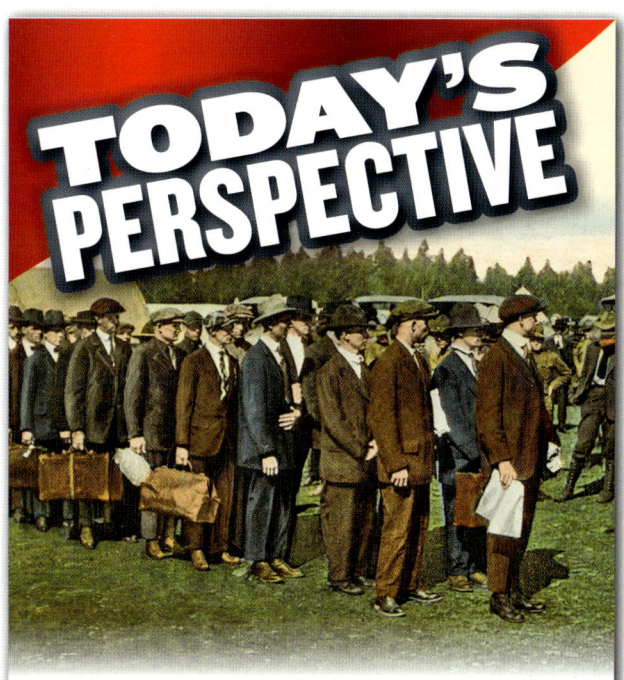

TODAY'S PERSPECTIVE

The U.S. government first used conscription during the Civil War (1861–1865). Conscription also helped build the military during World War I, World War II (1939–1945), the Korean War (1950–1953), and the Vietnam War (1954–1975). Many U.S. citizens do not agree with conscription. Groups have protested each time it has been put into use. It is illegal to refuse to fight if a person is drafted into the military. But many people do not believe in combat or support certain wars.

During the recent wars in Afghanistan and Iraq, some leaders proposed using conscription again. It did not happen, but it remains a possibility for any future conflicts.

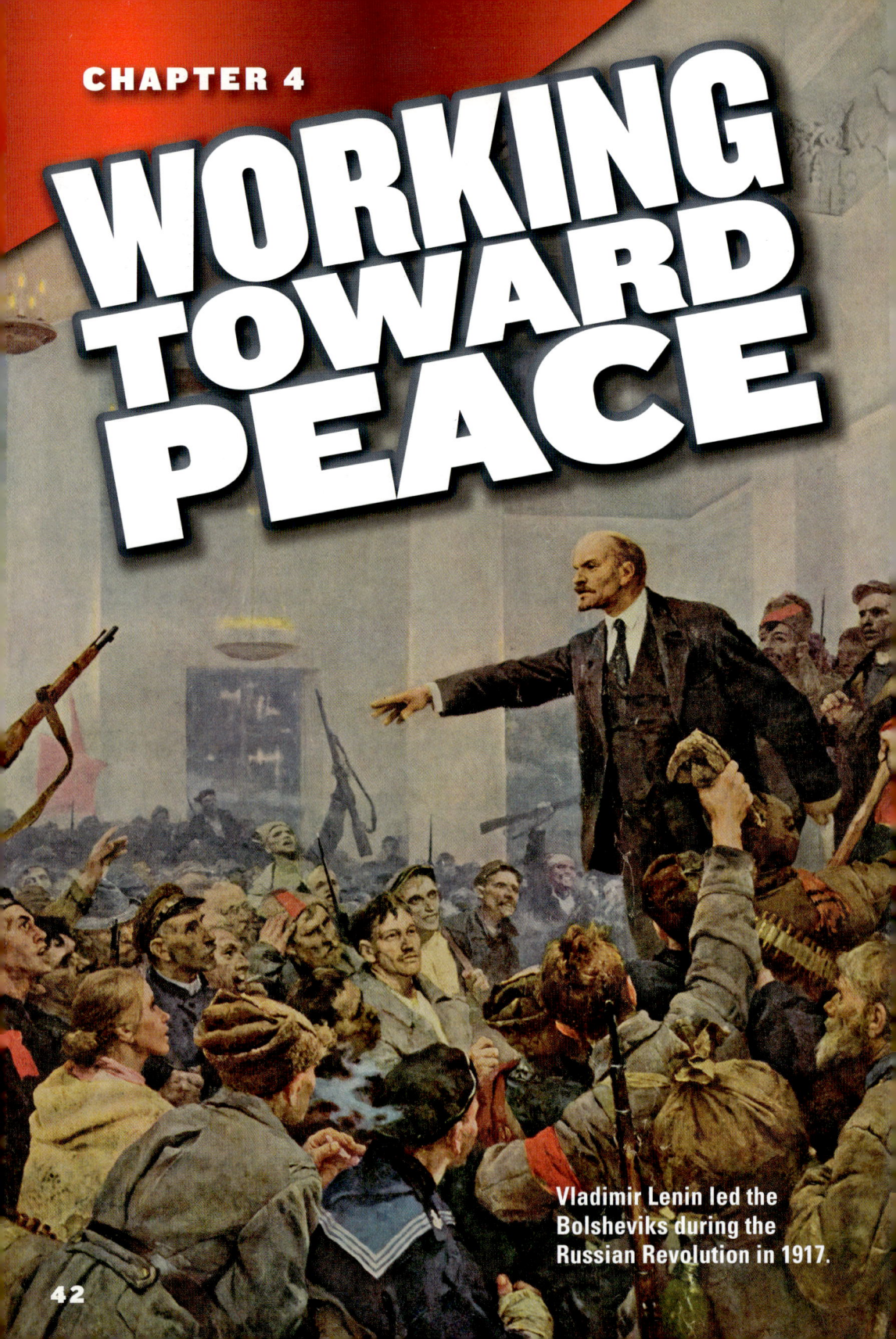

CHAPTER 4

WORKING TOWARD PEACE

Vladimir Lenin led the Bolsheviks during the Russian Revolution in 1917.

NOVEMBER 1917 SAW ANOTHER major change in the Russian government. The Bolshevik wing of the Russian Social-Democratic Workers' Party led a revolution against Russia's temporary government. Vladimir Lenin was the Bolsheviks' leader. One of the group's aims was to pull Russia out of the war. The war had caused major problems for the Russian economy. The Bolsheviks saw peace as the first step in rebuilding the nation. The new government began peace efforts almost immediately after taking power. They signed an **armistice** with Germany on December 15.

The Treaty of Brest-Litovsk ended the war on the eastern front.

The Fourteen Points and the Treaty of Brest-Litovsk

On January 8, 1918, President Wilson issued his Fourteen Points for a peaceful end to the war. They contained ideas for preventing such a major conflict from occurring again. They also outlined his ideas about which territories should be given to which nations.

On March 3, Russia and the Central powers signed a treaty in Brest-Litovsk. To achieve peace as soon as possible, the new Russian government was willing to cooperate with many of the Central powers' requests.

It gave up control of several of the western and southern parts of Russia's empire. New governments were created for places such as Finland, Ukraine, and Poland. Russia also handed part of its empire over to Turkey. With that, the war on the eastern front ended.

Action on the Western Front

With Russia out of the war, Germany was free to focus its efforts on the western front. On March 21, it began a major attack on French and British forces in northeast France. German general Erich Ludendorff hoped to move large numbers of German troops from the eastern front to the western front before American forces began arriving in significant numbers.

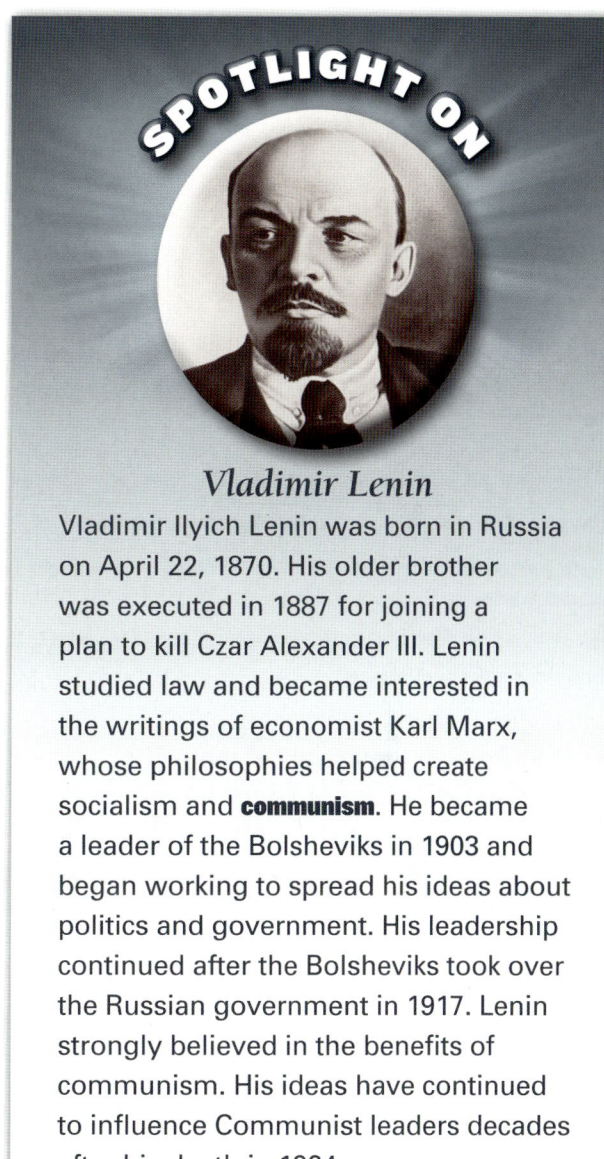

SPOTLIGHT ON

Vladimir Lenin

Vladimir Ilyich Lenin was born in Russia on April 22, 1870. His older brother was executed in 1887 for joining a plan to kill Czar Alexander III. Lenin studied law and became interested in the writings of economist Karl Marx, whose philosophies helped create socialism and **communism**. He became a leader of the Bolsheviks in 1903 and began working to spread his ideas about politics and government. His leadership continued after the Bolsheviks took over the Russian government in 1917. Lenin strongly believed in the benefits of communism. His ideas have continued to influence Communist leaders decades after his death in 1924.

His plan was fairly successful at first. By March 27, the Germans had pushed the Allied forces back about 40 miles (64 km). There were heavy losses on both sides. Ludendorff launched another attack against British forces on April 9 and continued pushing forward little by little. The Germans were able to continue this forward movement for several months. But such action was costly. They lost about 800,000 troops by mid-July. At the same time, the Allies were getting around 300,000 U.S. reinforcements each month.

The German offensive campaign came to an end with the Second Battle of the Marne in July. Germany began a series of attacks along the Marne River on July 15. But

Hundreds of thousands of men were killed or injured during the German offensive in early 1918.

Artillery helped the Allies push the Germans back during the Second Battle of the Marne.

the Allies were prepared. They put up heavy resistance and began a counteroffensive of their own. The German army soon began to fall apart. By September, the Germans had been pushed back to where they were at the beginning of the year. The Allies kept on the offensive throughout September and continued to wear down the Central powers. By early October, German military officers had begun asking the country's leaders to seek peace. The German military was too damaged to have any real chance at victory.

Unhappy German soldiers rebelled against their government during the revolution in 1918.

Peace at Last

German leaders began discussing peace with the Allied forces in October. But fighting continued as the peace talks began. German soldiers openly rebelled against orders to fight battles that the soldiers knew they would lose. On October 29, a naval **mutiny** sparked a revolution that quickly spread throughout the country. By November 4, many Germans were in open rebellion against the government. A new government established itself on November 7. Kaiser Wilhelm II fled to the Netherlands on November 10 and officially gave up power on November 28.

The end of World War I combat occurred during this time period. Turkey agreed to an armistice on October 30. The Austrian armistice was signed on November 3. Finally, the new German government signed an armistice with the Allies on November 11. Troops from around the world began returning to their home countries just a few weeks later.

The Paris Peace Conference began as leaders from the Allied nations started arriving in France in January 1919. In March, they decided that four leaders—Woodrow Wilson of the United States, David Lloyd George of Great Britain, Georges Clemenceau of France, and Vittorio Orlando of Italy—would handle

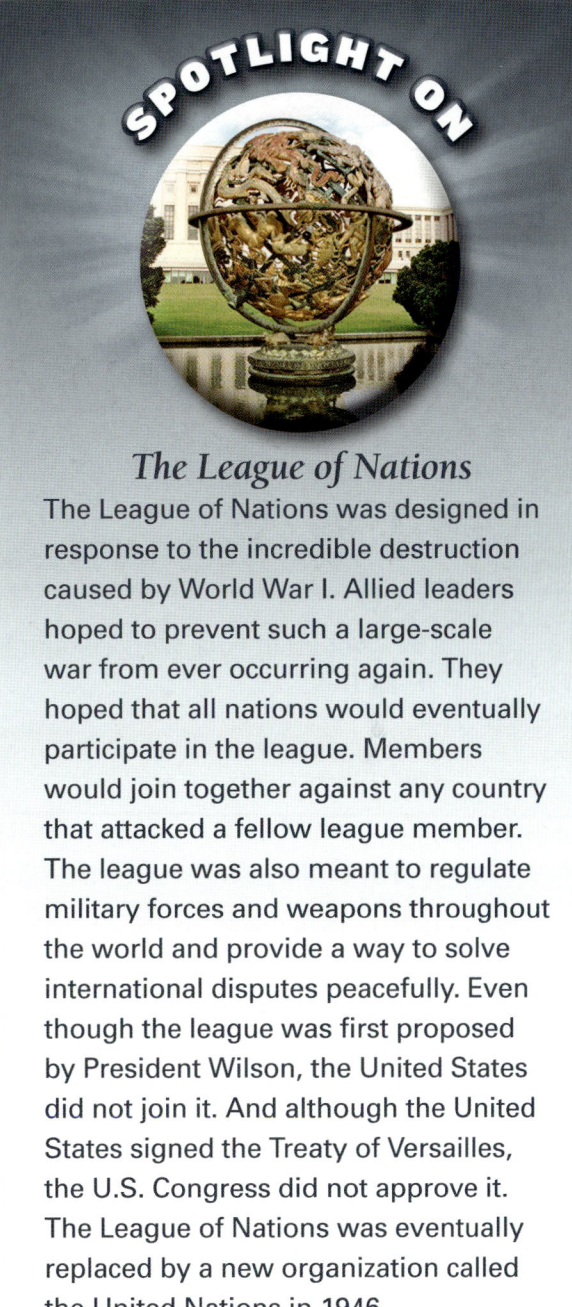

SPOTLIGHT ON

The League of Nations

The League of Nations was designed in response to the incredible destruction caused by World War I. Allied leaders hoped to prevent such a large-scale war from ever occurring again. They hoped that all nations would eventually participate in the league. Members would join together against any country that attacked a fellow league member. The league was also meant to regulate military forces and weapons throughout the world and provide a way to solve international disputes peacefully. Even though the league was first proposed by President Wilson, the United States did not join it. And although the United States signed the Treaty of Versailles, the U.S. Congress did not approve it. The League of Nations was eventually replaced by a new organization called the United Nations in 1946.

The Council of Four worked together to create the Treaty of Versailles.

the major decisions. Other leaders would also participate when necessary. This "Council of Four" worked to develop a peace plan that would protect the world against future conflicts. One of its ideas was to create a League of Nations. The league would allow representatives from countries around the world to monitor international affairs.

Treaties

On June 28, Germany and the Allies signed the Treaty of Versailles, marking the official end of the war. It was based largely on the ideas President Wilson had put forth in his Fourteen Points. The treaty contained a "war guilt clause" that declared Germany the main cause of the war. As a result, many of the treaty's points were very unfavorable to Germany. All conquered land was returned to France, Denmark, and Belgium. Poland was made an independent nation. All of Germany's colonies were divided up among the Allies.

Germany was also ordered to pay **reparations** for the damage caused by the war. The Allies set this amount at $33 billion in 1921. Germany was to be punished if it failed to make payments on this massive sum. Germany's military was also crippled. The army was reduced to just 100,000 men. The production of weapons such as tanks, airplanes, and poison gas was forbidden. Finally, Germany was no longer allowed to have a military presence in the western part of its own country.

The Allies signed a separate treaty with Austria on September 10. It broke up the Austro-Hungarian Empire. Czechoslovakia, Hungary, and Yugoslavia became independent nations. Austria was also forced to give up control of many colonies and other land holdings. Its military was reduced to 30,000 soldiers, and its navy was broken apart. Austrian ships were divided among the Allies. Like Germany, Austria was required by its treaty to pay reparations, but they were never actually paid. At long last, the war was over.

A FIRSTHAND LOOK AT
THE TREATY OF VERSAILLES

The Treaty of Versailles achieved peace between the Allies and Germany. It also punished Germany heavily for its role in the war. See page 60 for a link to read the full text of the treaty online.

What Happened Where?

ATLANTIC
OCEAN

North
Sea

NORW
O

UNITED
KINGDOM

DENMAR
Copenha

NETHERLANDS

London ⭐

⭐ Amsterdam

GERMA

BELGIUM

⭐ Brussels

Luxemb
LUXEMB

Somme R.

Marne R.

Paris ⭐

● Verdun

FRANCE

Bern ⭐

SWITZERLAND

ITA

Rome ⭐

Mediterranean Sea

Somme River The campaign along the Somme resulted in hundreds of thousands of casualties. The Allies only gained about 5 miles (8 km) of territory from the German forces.

Paris, France The Paris Peace Conference was held in Paris, France, in 1919. Decisions made there led to the unstable peace that ended World War I. The Versailles Treaty between the Allied powers and Germany was signed not far from Paris. The conference also created the League of Nations, which would eventually become the United Nations.

Marne River Two important battles were fought along the Marne River. In 1914, the first battle pushed back German forces in France and established the first trenches of the war. In 1918, Allied troops again held back a German offensive.

Verdun, France The fortresses located in Verdun formed a barrier between enemy armies and the French capital of Paris. In 1916, Verdun was the site of the single longest battle of World War I.

SWEDEN

★ Stockholm

★ Petrograd
(St. Petersburg)

Baltic Sea

RUSSIAN
EMPIRE

N
W E
S

| 0 | 200 | 400 mi |
| 0 | 200 | 400 km |

Vienna AUSTRIA-
★   HUNGARY

★ Budapest

MONTENEGRO

ROMANIA

Sarajevo ★ Bucharest
●   Belgrade
★

*Black
Sea*

Cetinje BULGARIA
★ ★ Sofia

ALBANIA SERBIA
Tirana ★

★ Constantinople
(Istanbul)

GREECE *Dardanelles*

OTTOMAN EMPIRE

★ Athens

Sarajevo, Bosnia Archduke Franz Ferdinand
was assassinated in Sarajevo, setting off an
international conflict that would escalate into
World War I.

Dardanelles Great Britain and France began
their naval attack against Turkey in the
Dardanelles channel in February 1915.

	Allied powers
	Central powers
	Neutral countries

Mediterranean Sea

A Changed World

The Treaty of Versailles ended the war, but it did not bring about a permanent peace.

The war's effect on the world did not end with the signing of the treaties. Even with combat concluded, the war continued to have a major impact on global politics. Russia and Germany had both experienced revolutions. Several new countries had been formed by the breaking

ADOLF HITLER RECEIVED MEDALS

up of the Russian and Austro-Hungarian Empires. It would take years for Europe to stabilize after these major developments.

In addition, the peace that followed the war would not last long. In choosing to punish Germany so severely, the Allies had unknowingly planted the seeds that would grow to become World War II. Germany's economy was weakened by the costs of reparations and the loss of territory. This caused dissatisfaction among the German people. A new leader named Adolf Hitler began using this unhappiness to gain support soon after the conclusion of World War I. He took control of Germany in 1933 and soon established himself as **dictator**. The flaws in the Allies' plan for peace were soon made clear to the world as Hitler and his Nazi Party led the world into violence once more.

Adolf Hitler's rise to power eventually led to the outbreak of World War II.

FOR BRAVERY DURING WORLD WAR I.

INFLUENTIAL INDIVIDUALS

Woodrow Wilson

Georges Clemenceau (1841–1929) was the French premier during World War I. His leadership helped bring the Allies to victory.

Helmuth von Moltke (1848–1916) was the German general whose decision to change the Schlieffen Plan was blamed for Germany's early failings in the war.

Woodrow Wilson (1856–1924) was the U.S. president during World War I. At first, he worked to keep the United States out of the war. He later chose to enter the fight after a series of aggressive actions by Germany.

Wilhelm II (1859–1941) was the ruler of Germany until the end of World War I. He was forced out of power by a German revolution in 1918.

Franz Ferdinand (1863–1914) was the heir to the Austrian throne whose assassination provided a reason for the early conflicts of the war.

David Lloyd George (1863–1945) became prime minister of Great Britain in 1916. His leadership helped the Allies achieve victory in the war.

Erich Ludendorff (1865–1937) was the general who led Germany's final offensive campaigns during the war.

Nicholas II (1868–1918) was the leader of Russia during the first years of the war. He was forced from power in 1917 and killed by revolutionaries in 1918.

Nicholas II

Vladimir Lenin (1870–1924) led the Bolshevik Revolution in 1917. His ideas about government and politics were a major influence throughout the following decades.

Vladimir Lenin

TIMELINE

1906

The European arms race intensifies when Great Britain constructs the HMS *Dreadnought*.

1912

Germany, Austria-Hungary, and Italy renew their Triple Alliance.

1914

June 28
Archduke Franz Ferdinand is assassinated.

July 23
Austria-Hungary issues an ultimatum to Serbia.

July 28
Austria-Hungary declares war on Serbia.

1915

May 23
Italy declares war on Austria-Hungary.

September 5
Czar Nicholas II takes over leadership of the Russian military.

1916

January
Great Britain begins its conscription program.

May 31
The Battle of Jutland begins.

July 1
The Somme campaign begins.

November 7
Woodrow Wilson is reelected president of the United States.

December 7
David Lloyd George is elected prime minister of Great Britain.

1914

August 1
Germany declares war on Russia.

August 3
Germany declares war on France and invades Belgium.

August 5–28
Montenegro, Great Britain, Serbia, and Japan enter the war.

August 26
The Battle of Tannenberg begins.

September
The war's first trenches are dug along the western front.

November
Russia declares war on Turkey.

1915

February
The Dardanelles Campaign begins.

April 26
The Treaty of London is signed.

May 7
German U-boats attack and sink the *Lusitania*.

1917

March
The Russian Revolution begins.

April 6
The United States declares war on Germany.

November
The Bolshevik Revolution results in a new Russian government.

1918

March 3
Russia and the Central powers sign the Treaty of Brest-Litovsk.

March 21
Germany begins its final offensive campaign.

November 7
A revolution in Germany results in a new German government.

1919

June 28
Germany and the Allied powers sign the Treaty of Versailles.

LIVING HISTORY

Primary sources provide firsthand evidence about a topic. Witnesses to a historical event create primary sources. They include autobiographies, newspaper reports of the time, oral histories, photographs, and memoirs. A secondary source analyzes primary sources, and is one step or more removed from the event. Secondary sources include textbooks, encyclopedias, and commentaries.

Austria-Hungary's Ultimatum The event that caused the war made headlines around the world. You can view the original news article about the ultimatum that appeared in the *New York Times* by visiting *www.nytimes.com/learning/general/onthisday/big/0723.html*

The Treaty of Versailles The Treaty of Versailles was a highly influential document in the first half of the 20th century. It ended the conflict with Germany in World War I, but it also set in motion events that would lead to World War II. You can read the full text of the treaty by visiting *http://avalon.law.yale.edu/subject_menus /versailles_menu.asp*

Truman's World War I Letters Future U.S. president Harry S. Truman enlisted in the military as soon as the United States entered World War I. He was shipped overseas in 1918 and served in the trenches during the final months of the war. You can read his letters home by visiting *www.trumanlibrary.org/whistlestop/study _collections/personal/large/ww1_letters/ww1_letters.htm*

World War I Photos Photos offer a close-up view of what life was like for the millions of men who served in the war. You can view a variety of World War I photos online by visiting *www.english .illinois.edu/maps/ww1/photoessay.htm*

Books

Bausum, Ann. *Unraveling Freedom: The Battle for Democracy on the Home Front During World War I.* Washington, DC: National Geographic, 2010.

Heinrichs, Ann. *Voices of World War I: Stories from the Trenches.* Mankato, MN: Capstone Press, 2011.

Marsico, Katie. *Woodrow Wilson.* New York: Marshall Cavendish Benchmark, 2011.

Perritano, John. *World War I.* New York: Franklin Watts, 2010.

Turner, Jason. *World War I, 1914–1918.* Mankato, MN: Black Rabbit Books, 2009.

Vander Hook, Sue. *The United States Enters World War I.* Edina, MN: ABDO Publishing, 2010.

Venezia, Mike. *Woodrow Wilson.* New York: Children's Press, 2007.

Web Sites

National WWI Museum
www.theworldwar.org/
View photos of World War I museum exhibits and find out how you can visit the museum for yourself.

PBS—The Great War and the Shaping of the 20th Century
www.pbs.org/greatwar/
Check out maps, photos, and comments from historians to learn more about World War I.

Visit this Scholastic Web site for more information on World War I:
www.factsfornow.scholastic.com

GLOSSARY

alliances (uh-LYE-uhns-iz) agreements to work together for some result

armistice (AHR-mi-stis) a temporary agreement to stop a war

artillery (ahr-TIL-uh-ree) large weapons that are fired from a distance

assassinate (uh-SASS-uh-nate) to murder, usually someone well known

blockade (blok-ADE) a closing off of an area, such as a port, to keep supplies from going in or out

casualties (KAZH-oo-uhl-teez) people killed or wounded during warfare

communism (KAHM-yuh-niz-uhm) a way of organizing the economy of a country so that all the land, property, businesses, and resources belong to the government or community, and the profits are shared by all

conscription (kun-SKRIP-shuhn) a program requiring men to join the military

dictator (DIK-tay-tur) a ruler who has complete control of a country, often by force

fronts (FRUHNTS) the areas where armies meet to fight

infantry (IN-fuhn-tree) soldiers who fight on foot

mutiny (MYOO-tuh-nee) revolt against authority, especially in the military

reparations (rep-uh-RAY-shuhnz) money paid to cover damages caused by war, supplied by the losing country

stalemate (STALE-mate) a position or situation that results in a deadlock, with no progress possible

trenches (TRENCH-iz) long, narrow ditches used to protect soldiers in battle

ultimatum (uhl-tuh-MAY-tuhm) a final offer or demand, especially one that carries with it the threat of punishment or the use of force if rejected

INDEX

Page numbers in *italics* indicate illustrations.

Alexander III, emperor of Russia, 45

Alexandra, empress of Russia, 31, 37

Allies, 12, 19, 21, 25, 27, 28, 33, *36*, 40–41, 46, 47, *47*, 48, 49, 50, 51, 52, *52–53*, 55, 56, 57

armistice, 43, 49

Austria-Hungary, 7, 12, 13, 14, 15–16, 17, 19, 21, 28, 49, 51, *53*, 55, 56

Belgium, 18–19, *18*, 23, 24, 51, *52*

Bolshevik Revolution, *42*, 43, 57

Bolsheviks, *42*, 43, 45, 57

Bosnia, 14, *14*, 53, *53*

casualties, 14, *14*, 26, *26*, 27, 29, 30, 33, 35, 36–37, 39, 46, *46*, 52, 57

Central powers, 19, 21, 41, 44, 47, *52–53*

Clemenceau, Georges, 49–50, 56

colonies, 6–7, *6*, *7*, 51

Czechoslovakia, 51

Dardanelles campaign, 27, 53, *53*

Denmark, 35, 51, *52*

economies, 6, 11, 39, 41, 43, 51, 55

First Battle of the Marne, 23, 24, *24*, 52, *52*

France, 6, 7, *7*, 11, 12, 17, 18, 19, 21, 22, 23, 24, *24*, 25, 27, 34, *34*, 35, 36, 37, 41, 45, 49–50, 51, 52, *52*, 53, 56

Franz Ferdinand, archduke of Austria, 14–15, *14*, *15*, 53, 56

George, David Lloyd, 37, 49–50, 57

Germany, 6, 7, 10–11, *11*, 12, *12*, 15, 17, 18–19, *18*, *20*, 21, 22, 23, 24, 25, 26, 27, 28, *28*, 29, 30, 34, *34*, 35, 36, 37, 38, 40, 43, 45, 46, *46*, 47, 48, *48*, 49, 50–51, 52, *52*, 54, 55, 56, 57

Great Britain, 6, *6*, 7, *8*, 10, 11, 12, 18, 19, 21, 24, *24*, 27, *28*, 29, *32*, 33, 35, 36–37, *36*, 38, 45, 46, 49–50, 52, 53, 57

Hitler, Adolf, 54–55, *55*

HMS *Dreadnought* (battleship), 10, *10*

Italy, 7, 12, 13, 19, 28, 49–50, *52–53*

Japan, 19

League of Nations, 49, *49*, 50, 52

Lenin, Vladimir Ilyich, *42*, 43, 45, *45*, 57, *57*

map, *52–53*

Montenegro, 13, 19, *53*

Nazi Party, 55

Nicholas II, emperor of Russia, *30*, 31, 37, 39–40, 57, *57*

Paris Peace Conference, 49–50, *50*, 52, *52*

Poland, 6–7, 45, 51
Rasputin, Grigory Yefimovich,
31, *31*, 37
RMS *Lusitania* (passenger ship),
28, 29, 30
Russia, 6–7, 12, 15, 17, 18, 19, 21,
25, 26, *26*, 27, *30*, 31, *31*, 37,
39–40, *39*, *42*, 43, 44, *44*, 45,
53, 54, 55, 57

Sarajevo, Bosnia, 14, *14*, 53, *53*
Second Battle of the Marne,
46–47, *47*, 52
Serbia, 13–14, 15–16, *16*, 17, *17*,
19, *53*
Somme campaign, 36–37, 52, *52*
SS *Arabic* (passenger ship), 29,
30

tanks, 37, 51
Treaty of Brest-Litovsk, 44–45, *44*
Treaty of London, 28
Treaty of Versailles, 49, 50–51,
50, 52, *54*
trenches, 25, *25*, 27, 36, *36*, 40,
52
Truman, Harry S., 40
Turkey, 13, *13*, 15, 27, 45, 49, 53

United Nations, 49, 52
United States, 29, 30, 37, 38–39,
40–41, *40*, 45, 46, 49–50, 56

Wilhelm II, emperor of Germany,
12, 15, 48, 56
Wilson, Woodrow, 29, 37, 38, *38*,
40, 44, 49–50, *50*, 56, *56*
World War II, 41, 55, *55*

ABOUT THE AUTHOR

Josh Gregory writes and edits books for kids. He lives in Chicago, Illinois.